SAINT-PETERSBURG

Peterhof · Tsarskoye Selo · Pavlovsk

181 colour plates

ALFA-COLOUR

Vladimir Krakovsky and Oleg Popov:
computer layout, 1998

ISBN 5-900959-16-3

PRINTED AND BOUND IN FINLAND

*The establishment of a new capital
of the Russian state at the place where
the Neva empties itself into the Baltic
Sea was historically predetermined.
By the late seventeenth century Russia
had grown rather strong and urgently
needed a sea route to Europe. Peter
the Great was attracted to the north-
western lands around the Gulf of
Finland which had once belonged to
Novgorod the Great, but later were
occupied by Sweden. Thus the
Northern War of 1700–21 between
Russia and Sweden for the domination
over the outlet to the Baltic broke out.*

*Peter the Great sought to
strengthen Russia's domination in
the area recovered from the Swedes.
An isle in the estuary of the Neva,
known as Hare's Island, was chosen
by the Tsar and his companion-in-
arms for the construction of a citadel
because its dominating position was
very suitable. The date of the
foundation of the St Petersburg
Fortress (later known as the Peter and
Paul Fortress), 16 (27 Old Style) May
1703 has been taken to be the day of
the establishment of St. Petersburg.
Near the fortress, under its coverage,
the construction of dwelling houses
began in the nearby area known as the
Petrograd Side now. The Tsar's closest
associates built their houses there.
A log house erected for the Tsar,
became Peter's earliest dwelling in
St Petersburg. In the area of Trinity
Square, the first square of the newly
built city, a shopping arcade was
erected; a sea port was established
nearby.*

*Under the pressure of Peter's
indomitable will the citadel city was
rapidly growing. Workers, soldiers
and serf peasants were brought here*

**Benoît Coffre. *Portrait of Peter
the Great.* The Great Palace, Peterhof**

View of the Winter Palace from Palace Square.
Watercolour by Vasily Sadovnikov. The Hermitage Museum

from all over Russia. The Tsar himself did not refuse to do any work. The efforts of the entire country were concentrated on the construction of the young capital. Peter the Great issued a decree which forbade any masonry construction elsewhere in Russia — all building materials were to be sent to St Petersburg.

Peter the Great wanted to create a powerful national fleet within a very short period. With this aim in view he laid out a shipyard, known as the Admiralty, on the left bank, diagonally from the St Petersburg Fortress downstream the Neva, in the autumn of 1704. Its general U-shaped plan was sketched by the Tsar himself, who had studied fortification and shipbuilding in West Europe.

The Tsar conceived the centre of the city on Vasilyevsky Island which was located near the sea. And since this part of the city was especially subject to floods, he ordered to carry out a

huge amount of work — to have the entire island cut with a network of straight canals. Although the canals were later filled in, Peter's decree has determined the unusual present-day layout of Vasilyevsky Island, with its three parallel prospects crossed by numerous straight streets or "lines". Later the Tsar ordered the port and the custom-house to be transferred to the island too. Major buildings of the government, such as the premises of the ministries, the Twelve Collegia, were also constructed there.

To build and decorate the new capital, Peter the Great invited all kinds of specialists — architects, engineers, painters, woodcarvers and sculptors. Thus, in 1703 Domenico Trezzini, an architect, engineer and specialist in fortification, came from Italy. He was responsible for the construction of all major structures in St Petersburg in the first quarter of the eighteenth century, including the

SS Peter and Paul Cathedral.

After the death of Peter the Great on 28 January of 1725 and especially from 1728, when the court returned to Moscow, St Petersburg began to lose its splendour, the construction slowed down and then ceased completely.

When Anna Ivanovna, Peter's niece, ascended the throne, the court was again returned to St Petersburg. To maintain her reputation as the follower of Peter the Great, the Empress did much to resume the construction in the northern capital. This period saw the creative activities of the Russian architects Mikhail Zemtsov, Piotr Yeropkin and Ivan Korobov. In the 1730s the scheme of the central part of the city, with a trident of its main thoroughfares, Nevsky Prospect, Voznesensky Prospect and Gorokhovaya Street, converging by the Admiralty, was formed.

A beautiful chapter in the history

View of the Winter Palace and the Neva Embankment in Winter. 1850s.
Lithograph after a drawing by Joseph Charlemagne

The Beloselsky-Belozersky Palace. 1850s. Lithograph after a drawing by Joseph Charlemagne

Show-Booths near the Admiralty during the Shrovetide. 1850s.
Lithograph after a drawing by Joseph Charlemagne

of St Petersburg is associated with the name of Francesco Bartolomeo Rastrelli, who used his outstanding talent to transform the city built on marshes into a majestic ensemble of royal and aristocratic residences. Inspired in his childhood by the luxury of Versailles, Rastrelli succeeded in combining a refined European spirit with traditions of Russian national architecture, being not indifferent to its sensual, highly individual beauty. The façades of Rastrelli's resplendent edifices — the Smolny Cathedral and the Winter Palace, as well as the Stroganov, Great Peterhof and Catherine Palaces — still largely determine the appearance of the centre of St Petersburg and its environs today.

The luxurious Baroque that flourished in the age of Elizabeth Petrovna, was replaced by the austere grandeur and noble simplicity of Classicism. Although both periods have yielded fine examples of architecture without which the appearance of the northern capital cannot be imagined now, it is generally believed that the essence of St Petersburg as a unique architectural phenomenon lies in its Classical buildings. The flowering of Russian Classicism is deservedly associated with the glorious age of Catherine the Great who tended towards the ideas of the Enlighteners with their revived interest in Classical Antiquity. The beautiful buildings put up by Antonio Rinaldi, Jean-Baptiste Vallin de la Mothe, Alexei Kokorinov, Yury Velten, Ivan Starov, Giacomo Quarenghi and other Classicist architects radically changed the appearance of Peter's city.

Classicism introduced new aesthetic guidelines and brought a revival of an interest in urban building and ensemble construction, spectacular examples of which were created in the first decades of the nineteenth century by Andreyan Zakharov, Andrei Voronikhin and Jean-François Thomas de Thomon. They set the trend for the architects active after the War of 1812 — for Vasily Stasov, Auguste de Montferrand and Alexander Briullov. But it is to the architectural genius of Carlo Rossi that we owe the creation of some most outstanding St Petersburg ensembles — Palace Square with the Arch of the General Staff building, Senate Square completed by the building of the Senate and Holy Synod, Mikhailovskaya Square with the Mikhailovsky Palace dominating it, the complex of the Alexandrine Theatre with the unique Rossi Street.

The Beloselsky-Belozersky Palace. 1850s.
Lithograph after a drawing by Joseph Charlemagne

The inevitable process of Russia's industrialization, which began in the middle of the nineteenth century, considerably increased the scope of architectural work. The growth of population stimulated dwelling construction. In the same way as in other European capitals, large houses for many families began to dominate in urban residential building. New types of public structures — railway stations, markets and shops — began to appear. New functions determined the introduction of new engineering solutions and building materials.

In connection with these developments Classicist aesthetics underwent a certain change loosing its harmonious clarity and austerity of shapes characteristic of High Classicism. The complex of buildings erected on St Isaac's Square was one of the last examples of a large-scale architectural and spatial project.

An interest in the styles of the past began to be keenly felt and retrospective features grew more prominent in architecture. Majestic works by Andrei Stakenschneider are illustrious examples of this trend.

In the second half of the nineteenth and early twentieth centuries the panorama of the Neva and other waterways completely changed. New embankments were faced with granite and bridge-building was making a rapid progress. The Annunciation (Nikolayevsky), Liteiny, Trinity and Large Okhta Bridges were constructed; the Palace Bridge began to function. The introduction of railways communication led to the building of stations, and the erection of platforms for them resulted in the use of progressive up-to-date technologies.

The so-called Neo-Russian Style became then widely popular. Its features can be felt in the Cathedral of the Resurrection (commonly known as "Our Saviour-on-the-Spilt-Blood") which has been recently opened after restoration. This ornate, fanciful building is in marked contrast to the Classical ensembles in the central part of the city and introduces a touch of the mediaeval, Muscovite tradition into the Europeanized St Petersburg style.

There are many impressive Art Nouveau examples in the city. The fanciful decor and emphasized compositional misbalance of early-twentieth-century structures by Fiodor Lidval, Pavel Suzor and Alexander von Gogen have added a special accent to St Petersburg enriching its image as a brilliant European city.

Panorama of the Peter and Paul Fortress

The Peter Gate of the Peter and Paul Fortress. 1717–18
Architect Domenico Trezzini

The initial core around which St Petersburg centred was **the Peter and Paul Fortress**. The choice of Hare Island for the building of fortified structures was extremely happy, since it provided a fine commanding view of the Small and Large Nevas. Moreover, a small size of the river island enabled to accommodate all necessary structures without leaving a strip along the bank where an enemy could make a landing. About twenty thousand workers were employed daily to strengthen the marshy grounds and to erect earthen ramparts. They were supervised by Peter's associates Menshikov, Golovkin, Zotov, Trubetskoi and Naryshkin, whose names were given to fortress bastions, and one was named after the Tsar himself. The fortress, built in keeping with the latest achievement in the European art of fortification, was designed to withstand contemporary artillery — hexagonal in plan, with fortified bastions at the corners linked by curtain walls. Its gates were

View of the Peter and Paul Fortress from the Trinity Bridge

The Peter Gate of the Peter and Paul Fortress. 1717–18
Architect Domenico Trezzini

Monument to Peter the Great. 1991. Sculptor Mikhail Chemiakine

additionally strengthened with ravelins, moats were dug out and spanned with drawbridges.

The walls of the citadel are amazingly thick. For example the Neva Curtain Wall is 12 metres high and 2.5 metres thick. The walls of the Tsar's and Naryshkin Bastions are about 4 metres thick. They could undoubtedly stand the assault of an enemy, but it happened so that the Peter and Paul Fortress was never tested in battle. However, every day at noon a cannon shot can be heard from its bastion by inhabitants of the city and its guests. This distinct St Petersburg tradition has been maintained for many decades thus setting a tune for the varied gamut of urban sounds. In past times, however, a salvo from the Naryshkin Bastion could throw a crowd into a panic — it not only signalled the midday but was also used as an alarm to warn people that the level of water in the Neva was rising and there was a danger of a flood.

In 1787 work on the facing the curtain walls and bastions was finished. The walls were "clad in stone" from the river side, at the length of 700 metres. Nowadays, as early as March, with the first warm rays of sunlight, the fortress walls are often stormed — not by an enemy, of course, but by those who want to get sun-burnt. The granite accumulating warmth creates a special climate which allows enthusiasts to have sun-baths even at that early spring time, which is not at all a warm season in this northern land, with the snow still not melting.

Walking from the Tsar's Bastion along the Neva Curtain Wall, you will soon reach the Commandant's Pier decorated with **the Neva Gate**, remarkable for its harmonious simplicity and quiet balance. This is one of the most perfect examples of Early Classicism. Once a year, starting from the Petrine age, a solemn procession used to bring out Peter the Great's boat (also affectionately called "the grandfather of the Russian fleet"), place it on a barge and carry to the opposite bank of the Neva, to the St Alexander Nevsky Lavra

The Neva Gate of the Peter and Paul Fortress. 1784–87. Architect Nikolai Lvov

(major monastery); in the evening the boat was brought back. The ceremony was accompanied by gunfire and music performed by military orchestras.

The architectural effect produced by the Peter and Paul Fortress is based on the combination of the horizontal line of its walls and the vertical thrust of the bell-tower of the SS Peter and Paul Cathedral crowned with a tall spire.

The construction of the present-day **SS Peter and Paul Cathedral** began in 1712 under the guidance of Domenico Trezzini on the former site of a wooden church. The cathedral was finished already after Peter's death, in 1733, and consecrated to the Apostles Peter and Paul. Since the Emperor attached great importance to the bell-tower of the cathedral as a landmark of the newly built capital, it was constructed with a haste and completed ten years before the cathedral. Today the bell-tower of the SS Peter and Paul Cathedral still remains one of the tallest structures in the city punctuating the sky above it and second only to the TV tower built after the war. In 1833 the angel crowning the spire began to bend, but a certain Piotr Telushkin, showing a tremendous courage, endurance and sharpness of wit, saved it from falling. Using merely a rope he succeeded in climbing to the point of the spire and repairing the damaged figure within several weeks, free of charge. In the 1850s the spire was rebuilt and as a result it became 122.5 metres high.

The cathedral itself, like its bell-tower, was built in the traditions of the early, so-called Petrine, Baroque, which was not traditional for Russian church architecture. The building is unusually vast and filled with light and air. Its architectural details are painted to imitate marble, its moulding is gilded and its vaults are adorned with painting. The cathedral is used as the burial place of the royal family — all Emperors of Russia beginning with Peter the Great are buried there, except for Nicholas II.

Having won no glory in battle, the Peter and Paul Fortress became famous

The SS Peter and Paul Cathedral. 1712–33. Architect Domenico Trezzini

The Imperial Throne in the SS Peter and Paul Cathedral

Lectern in the SS Peter and Paul Cathedral

as the "Russian Bastille" — the most dangerous political prisoners were held in it. The first prisoner of the Peter and Paul Fortress was Peter the Great's son, Tsarevich Alexis, who became a victim and tool of opposition to his crowned father. The Neva Gate had an ill fame. During a night, under a shelter of darkness, those condemned to death were brought through the Commandant's Pier to ships which carried them away to the place where sentences were executed.

Tombs of Peter the Great and Catherine I in the SS Peter and Paul Cathedral

The Exchange. 1805–16. Architect Jean-François Thomas de Thomon

Allegorical figure of *The Volkhov River*
by the pedestal of the Rostral Column. 1810. By Samson Sukhanov

The largest island on the territory recovered from the Swedes and known as Vasilyevsky Island now, is remarkable for its long shore opening to the Gulf of Finland. The Tsar presented this island to his closest associate Alexander Menshikov, a hero of the Northern War and the first Governor General of St Petersburg. It was on Vasilyevsky Island and especially on its best part, commonly known as the Spit, that the administrative, scientific and trade centre of the capital was to be constructed.

As early as the 1780s a building of the Exchange, an edifice so necessary for fruitful contacts in interior and foreign trade, began to be erected at the Spit of Vasilyevsky Island, but the construction lingered for years and ended in failure. The task to turn the ensemble of the Spit

The Kunstkammer. 1718–34. Architects Georg Johann Mattarnovi, Nikolaus Härbel, Gaetano Chiaveri and Mikhail Zemtsov

Lion at the Palace Landing-Stage

into a regular and symmetrical composition was realized by the talented architect Jean-François Thomas de Tomon.

The building of **the Exchange** is modelled on a Classical temple. Its central volume, encircled with a Doric colonnade, is raised on a high granite stylobate with wide majestic stairways and gently sloping ramps leading to it. The sculptural groups located on the attics play an important role in the decor of the façades. The design of the Exchange included the construction of the so-called Rostral Columns to be used as lighthouses near the descends to the Neva. The pedestals and the columns themselves were decorated with *rostra*, or prows, imitating the beaks of captured ships. The huge figures placed by the columns symbolized Russian rivers — the Volga, Dnieper, Neva and Volkhov. The column tops were equipped with lamps which are nowadays provided with gas. On festive days torches of fire light up the sky above the columns.

Now the building of the Exchange houses the State Naval Museum.

Russia's first public museum, **the Kunstkammer**, or Cabinet of Curios, stands at the spot where the Spit turns into University Embankment. Peter the Great conceived it as a library and a collection of "monsters and rarities". His desire to educate the population was so strong that he ordered that anyone should be admitted to the Kunstkammer, given explanations and, moreover, one's

Unknown Russian artist. *Portrait of Alexander Menshikov*. **1716–20.
The Hermitage Museum**

interest in natural sciences should be encouraged by a cup of coffee or a glass of vodka.

The building also housed an anatomical theatre, while its tower contained the first Russian observatory and a large globe, a prototype of present-day planetarium. For a long time the Kunstkammer was the seat of the Academy of Sciences, where the great Russian scientist Mikhail Lomonosov worked. Now the building houses the Museum of Ethnography and Anthropology.

The Kunstkammer is an interesting example of the Petrine Baroque — the façade of the building is articulated with white pilaster strips and panels contrasting with the blue of the walls; the corners of projections are rusticated. The four-tiered tower crowned with a sphere lends a particularly dynamic appearance to the building. **The palace of Alexander Menshikov**, one of the earliest masonry buildings in St Petersburg, is also located on the University Embankment. Menshikov was one of the most striking personalities in Russian history. Springing from a low social group, he achieved the status of the second person in the state. Peter distinguished him as none around him for his wit, bravery and cheerfulness revealed during the numerous battles of the Northern War, including the crucial battle of Poltava. No less appreciated was Menshikov's passion for their common

course — the creation of innovated Russia. These qualities overshadowed for the Emperor Menshikov's numerous faults, such as bribery, avarice and embezzlement of public funds. It was no secret for the Tsar that Menshikov often used the public purse as his own. Peter presented him with towns, plots of land, titles and orders. A portrait shows us this "spoiled child of fortune" in the glitter of his regalia at the culmination of his brilliant and dramatic career. After the death of his benefactor, it was Menshikov, a power behind the throne, rather than Empress Catherine I, who ruled Russia for three years. Even when he fell into disgrace and lost his huge wealth, Menshikov did not descend for an appeal to pardon him and ended his life in Siberian exile.

By its luxury and magnificenc the Menshikov Palace outshone all mansions of the nobility and even royal residences in the capital. Peter the Great used it to receive ambassadors and for parties, the more so as the owner was remarkable for his generosity and hospitality.

The four-storeyed palace, under a tall, pitched roof, struck by its dimensions as there was nothing comparable in St Petersburg at the time. Right near the porch there was a large wooden landing-stage painted in imitation of brick. Gondolas and boats with guests moored to it — at that time the Neva was very close to the building. The façades of the Menshikov Palace, remarkable for their unassuming decor, are typical of St Petersburg architecture of the early eighteenth century. As for the interiors of the palace, the entrance hall with ornate vaults, columns and sculpture in the niches is in a particularly good state of preservation, as are the so-called Barbara's Apartments, where Delft tiles are used not only to cover the walls from top to bottom in the Dutch fashion, but even to decorate the ceilings. Worthy of note on the upper storey of the palace is the Walnut Study where Menshikov usually received his crowned friend. Its walls are faced with finely patterned wood; the ceiling painting is also beautiful.

The Menshikov Palace. 1710–27. Architects Mario Giovanni Fontana and Johann Gottfried Schädel

The Great Chamber in the Menshikov Palace

**The Reception Room belonging to Varvara's Apartments
in the Menshikov Palace**

**The Walnut Study in the Menshikov Palace. 1716–18.
Architects Jean-Baptiste Le Blond (?) and Johann Gottfried Schädel**

Soon after Menshikov's fall the palace began to house a cadet corps. Many prominent figures in Russian culture studied there. Now the building of the Menshikov Palace is used as a branch of the Russian Department of the Hermitage Museum.

The building of **the Academy of Arts**, an outstanding example of the architecture of Early Classicism, completes the University Embankment. Its volumes are simple and concise, austere and at the same time unusually expressive. The four-columned portico in the centre of the building is decorated with the statues of *Hercules* and *Flora*.

The Kitchen in the Menshikov Palace

Detail of the interior of the Walnut Study in the Menshikov Palace

The Academy of Arts. 1764–68. Architects Alexei Kokorinov and Jean-Baptiste Vallin de la Mothe

Founded in 1757, the Academy played a very important role in the history of Russian fine arts. Many outstanding painters, sculptors and architects were its graduates.

The granite embankment opposite the Academy of Arts is decorated with granite sphinxes. The sphinxes, with the faces of Amenhotep III, are more than 3,000 years old. Once they guarded the burial tomb of the pharaoh. The sphinx, a mythological creature of Egyptian mythology, strong as a lion and clever as a man, was believed to safeguard tombs and temples from hostile forces. Now the stone effigies, which arrived

Sphinx at the landing-stage by the Academy of Arts

Monument to Ivan Krusenstern. 1870–73. Sculptor Ivan Schröder, architect Hyppolito Monighetti

to St Petersburg from hot Thebes, guard the granite St Petersburg embankment washed by the waters of the northern river.

You can feel a proximity of the sea on Vasilyevsky Island as nowhere else in the city. That part of the Lieutenant Schmidt Embankment where a **monument to Admiral Ivan Krusenstern**, head of the first Russian voyage around the world, stands, is pervaded with a romantic spirit of sea adventures. You can see a large variety of ships in this part of the Neva, including sailing boats with tall masts. Future naval officers set out for training cruises from this spot.

Peter's plans to make Vasilyevsky Island the centre of St Petersburg were not realized largely due to an isolated position of the island from the rest of the city and a lack of bridges. As a result the centre shifted to the left bank of the Neva, which was higher and less vulnerable to floods. Besides, all communications which connected the capital with central Russia, met near the Admiralty.

The Admiralty part of the city (the third to be populated, after Petrograd Side and Vasilyevsky Island), where the main palaces and most attractive buildings of the northern capital are situated, can be reached from the Spit of Vasilyevsky Island through the Palace Bridge. A small monument, *The Tsar-Shipwright*, stands not far from Palace Bridge. The sculpture shows the young Peter. The Tsar worked as a common apprentice at the shipyard in the Dutch town of Saardam — he learned to build ships by his own hands. The monument you can see today is a copy of the statue which had once stood on this site. Many years after the monument was lost, the government of the Netherlands has presented this copy to St Petersburg. The position near the former Admiralty shipyard where the monument now

Panoramic view of the Neva from the Kronwerk Strait

The Tsar-Shipwright. **1909. Sculptor Leopold Bernstamm**

Guns and cannon balls near the main entrance to the Admiralty

redesign it. In addition to the shipyard, it was planned to accommodate the Naval Ministry there, so the building was to have a more imposing appearance. The task of redesigning the shipyard was entrusted to Andreyan Zakharov, a leading architect of the period. It is interesting to note that two large-scale projects were undertaken simultaneously on both banks of the river — the building of the Exchange was being erected on the Spit of Vasilyevsky Island at the same time.

Zakharov had to take into consideration the specific character of the

The building of the Admiralty. 1806–23. Architect Andreyan Zakharov

Sculptural group *Sea Nymphs Carrying the Celestial Sphere* by the main gate of the Admiralty. 1812. Sculptor Theodosy Shchedrin

stands, is not a mere coincidence. Peter the Great placed great hopes on the Admiralty — it was established to build ships for the Northern War. Indeed, the numerous ships which descended from the stocks of the shipyard, determined the outcome of the war.

The building of the Main Admiralty dominates the centre of the city — Palace, Decembrists' and Senate Squares, and therefore it would be

reasonable to begin our sightseeing tour of the left bank of the Neva from it.

Many architects contributed to the construction of the Admiralty throughout the eighteenth century. The shipyard had a particularly ungainly look next to the splendid royal residence, the Winter Palace. In the early nineteenth century, taking into consideration the significance of the Admiralty as a landmark of the city, it was decided to

Panoramic view of the Winter Palace

Palace Square
The General Staff building. 1819–29. Architect Carlo Rossi

historically formed architectural landscape. The peculiar feature of the central part of St Petersburg was the predominance of the two spires — those of the SS Peter and Paul Cathedral and the Admiralty. It was towards the golden needle of the Admiralty that the famous "trident" of the three main streets of the city was oriented. So Zakharov repeated the major motif of the structure designed by his predecessor, Ivan Korobov, but made the spire of the new Admiralty half as tall again.

The principal difficulty Zakharov had was the length of the Admiralty

Bas-relief *Victory and History* on the pedestal of the Alexander Column. 1832. Sculptors Piotr Svintsov and Ivan Leppe

31

— the main façade stretches for 415 metres and each of the wings is 172 metres long. The pavilions facing the Neva are truly beautiful. Originally the entire building was enclosed with canals and the pavilions pierced with arches soared above them. Ships could enter the shipyard through the arched canals.

The central gate is flanked with magnificent sculptural groups of sea nymphs mounted on high granite pedestals and supporting celestial spheres. The Ionic colonnade is crowned with a cupola over which soars a spire with a famous weather-vane in the form of a ship, a symbol of St Petersburg (the height of the tower with the spire is 72.3 metres).

The magnificent panorama unfolding before your eyes from the *Bronze Horseman* towards the Admiralty façades is in full accord with the superb complex of buildings on Palace Square. This ensemble is one of the most impressive not only in Russian but in world architecture as well. Its notable feature is a perfect blend of the Baroque and Classical buildings — the two major styles which dominate the centre of the city. The complex of Palace Square is inseparably associated with the names of the celebrated St Petersburg architects — Francesco Bartolomeo Rastrelli and Carlo Rossi.

Miniature copy of the Imperial regalia. Late 19th century. Jeweller Karl Fabergé

The Main (Jordan) Staircase in the Winter Palace. 1762, architect Francesco Bartolomeo Rastrelli; 1831, architect Vasily Stasov

The "Large" Carriage. First quarter of the 18th century. France, Paris

**The Peter Room in the Winter Palace. 1833, architect Auguste de Montferrand;
1837–38, architect Vasily Stasov**

The Malachite Room in the Winter Palace. 1830, architect Auguste de Montferrand

The Winter Palace is the first edifice put up on Palace Square. It was erected by the great Rastrelli in the latter half of the reign of Empress Elizabeth Petrovna. The earlier Winter Palace had failed to accommodate the court and it was decided to put up a new building. The project of such a scale turned out to be difficult and the work lasted for many years. Elizabeth Petrovna did not get a chance to live in it — it was only after her death that Emperor Peter III moved to the still unfinished palace. Peter III, however, did not live long. In the summer of 1762 he was dethroned and killed in his country residence. The Winter Palace passed to Catherine the Great. During the first ten years of her rule the building was being finished and decorated inside. The palace was often the venue for luxurious balls and masquerades, which always attracted many people — for example, in 1772 twelve halls were at the disposal of guests.

The luxurious court life witnessed by the walls of the palace for thirty years, ended with the death of the Empress in November 1796.

Life at the court became much different in the reign of Paul I and later during the nineteenth century — the palace was now more often used for official ceremonies which had no splendour or luxury comparable to those of the eighteenth century.

The Winter Palace served as a residence of the Russian Tsars for a century and a half, until the revolution of 1917.

The devastating fire of 1837 totally destroyed the inner decor of the palace and left no trace of its former magnificence. The fire ravaged for three days. On 29 November 1837 a special commission was formed for the reconstruction of the palatial interiors. The architect Vasily Stasov was entrusted to restore the building and its outward decoration, as well as to redesign its two churches and state rooms, while Alexander Briullov was charged to decorate Nicholas I's private apartments and the Alexander Hall. The main condition set by the commission

Fiodor Rokotov. *Portrait of Catherine II. Ca.* **1770. The Hermitage Museum**

was that the majority of the palace should be recreated exactly as it had been before the fire, but it turned out that the task could not be fulfilled.

The main façade of the Winter Palace overlooks **Palace Square**. It is perhaps the most brilliant and impressive Baroque building in St Petersburg. The palace strikes viewers by its unusual integrity and beauty. The variety of decoration, lavish window surrounds, moulded decoration, sculptures, perfect grouping of columns and, finally, a vivid

combination of white and green colours — all these features serve to make this very long façade less monotonous. In the eighteenth and nineteenth centuries the Winter Palace served as a model for all other buildings in the city — none of them could be taller than the Winter Palace which was about 23 metres high.

The southern border of Palace Square is formed by the powerful curve of the buildings of **the General Staff and the Ministries** put up by Carlo Rossi between 1819 and 1829 in the manner

The Pavilion Hall in the Small Hermitage. 1850–58. Architect Andrei Stakenschneider

of Classicism. It is unequalled for length — its façade overlooking Palace Square stretches for some 580 metres and the other one, facing the Moika, is about 265 metres. The architect perfectly evaded the impression of monotony of the façades by placing the main accent on the triumphal arch. Majestic and at the same time clear-cut in its decor, this structure, crowned with a chariot of Victory driven by a group of horses, is neither too sumptuous nor excessively refined. It perfectly blends with the ensemble of Palace Square, and its restraint only stresses the luxury and magnificence of the Winter Palace.

The centrepiece of Palace Square is **the Alexander Column** set up to commemorate the victorious end of the War of 1812. Its powerful Doric shaft, carved of a huge granite monolith resting on a bronze base and decorated with ornate capital and bas-reliefs on the pedestal, is crowned with the figure of an angel.

The monument was carved from a granite monolith excavated at the Pyuterlaks quarry on the northern shore of the Gulf of Finland. The overall height of the monument from the pedestal to the angel at its top is 47.5 metres. It is the highest monolithic column in the world. On 30 August 1832, viewed by a huge crowd of people, the stone weighing 600 tons was winched to its position on the pedestal. The lifting lasted for 1 hour 45 minutes.

Leonardo da Vinci. 1452–1519
The Litta Madonna. **1490–91**

Leonardo da Vinci. 1452–1519
The Benois Madonna. **1478**

The building of the Guards Headquarters limits Palace Square from the east. Its construction began in 1837 to the design of Alexander Briullov and ended in 1843. The main façade decorated with a portico of twelve Ionic columns, is worthy of note for its classical proportions.

All the three edifices of Palace Square, created in different periods, are diverse in style, but they are inseparably linked in terms of space.

The northern façade of the Winter Palace overlooks the Neva. Here one of the most splendid embankments in St Petersburg, stretching from Palace Bridge to Trinity Bridge, begins. Its focal point is **the complex of buildings of the Hermitage Museum** including the Winter Palace which is ranked among the best palaces in Europe not only for the wealth of its architecture, but also for the luxury of its interior decor.

Already at the entrance hall a feeling of vastness and majesty overwhelms the visitor. The two long rows of white

The Leonardo da Vinci Room in the Old Hermitage. 1851–54. Architect Andrei Stakenschneider

Peter Paul Rubens. 1577–1640
The Union of Earth and Water. Ca. 1618

Rembrandt. 1606–1669
Danaë. **1640s**

columns form a sort of a gallery in the depth of which is a wide staircase, full of light and glistening with its gilded decor. This is the Main or Jordan Staircase. The Jordan Entrance on the side of the Palace Embankment was used on the Day of Baptism by the male members of the Imperial family and the highest clergy who went to the Neva where, on a special platform the water was sanctified under the accompaniment of salvoes from the Exchange on Vasilyevsky Island. During the reign of Nicholas II, the Winter Palace was used for annual balls usually held in January, one large-scale ball and two or three smaller festivals. Up to 5,000 guests were invited to the large ball centred in the Hall of St Nicholas.

One of the palace's interiors, the Peter the Great Hall, is dedicated to the memory of the founder of St Petersburg. The vaults here are painted with a gold pattern skilfully incorporating the crown, the double-headed eagles and the Latin monograms *PP* (*Petrus Primus*). In the depth of the hall is an allegorical formal portrait produced by the Italian eighteenth-century artist Jacopo Amiconi in 1731 and portraying Peter with the goddess of wisdom Minerva against the background of the sea and ships. The throne surmounted with the crown stands under the portrait. It was made in London in the early eighteenth century.

The decor of the state rooms and halls of the Winter Palace is amazing for its majesty and variety. Thus, in the Malachite Room, designed by Alexander Briullov, the columns, pilasters and fireplaces are faced with skilfully chosen plaques of green malachite brought from the Urals. The pattern of the parquet floor in this room is composed of precious kinds of wood, the ceiling and doors are adorned with gilded moulding.

43

Next to the Winter Palace stands the Small Hermitage built by the architect Jean-Baptiste Vallin de la Mothe in 1764–67 for Empress Catherine the Great. Here the paintings and sculptures kept in different rooms of the Winter Palace were brought together for the first time. In the eighteenth century it became known as the *hermitage*, or an abode of a recluse. Later the pavilion's name was used for the entire museum.

One of the most beautiful rooms in the Small Hermitage is the Pavilion Hall. It is remarkable for an abundance of light pouring in from numerous windows. Rays of light are refracted in crystal pendants of huge chandeliers sparkling with all the colours of the spectrum. There is something whimsical in the decor of this room reminiscent of fairy-tale palaces of eastern rulers. The fountains-shells placed by the walls also suggest an influence of an Oriental style.

A surprising bronze object, the *Peacock* clock, never fails to attract visitors' attention in this room. Its unusual dial is located on the top of a large mushroom; its slowly moving figures indicate hours and minutes. The clock was made by the English watchmaker James Cock and bought by Grigory Potiomkin as a present for Catherine the Great. It was assembled in Russia by the famous mechanic Ivan Kulibin.

Next to the Small Hermitage is a building representing a complex of structures erected in different periods and known as the Old (or Large) Hermitage, the block of Raphael's loggias which are a replica of the similarly named gallery in the Vatican

The Small Italian Skylight Hall in the New Hermitage. 1842–51. Architects Vasily Stasov and Nikolai Yefimov. Designed by Leo von Klenze

Detail of the interior of the Small Spanish Skylight Hall in the New Hermitage

Alfred Sisley. 1839–1899
Villeneuve-la-Garenne. 1872

Claude Monet. 1840–1926
Lady in the Garden

Palace in Rome, and the New Hermitage remarkable for its beautiful interior decor. The architectural complex of the museum also includes the building of the palace theatre, a splendid example of eighteenth-century theatrical architecture.

All the Hermitage buildings are linked by covered bridges or passageways which enable visitors to view its halls and rooms as parts of a single museum display.

The Department of Western European Painting, the oldest in the museum, occupies almost a half of the Hermitage display rooms.

The art of Italy is represented in the Hermitage by first-rate paintings. Among masterpieces of the fourteenth and fifteenth centuries are works by Simone Martini, Filipino Lippi and Perugino. The so-called Leonardo da Vinci Room features two outstanding works by the great master of the Italian Renaissance. These are *The Litta Madonna*, which bears the name of its former owners, the Milanese dukes of Litta, from whom it was bought for the Hermitage in 1865. Another work, *The Benois Madonna*, belonged to the Sapozhnikov family and was purchased by Emperor Nicholas II for the Hermitage collection in 1914 thanks to the efforts of Benois and other cultural figures.

The Hermitage collection of seventeenth-century Flemish painting includes works by all major masters of this school. But the pride of place belongs to Peter Paul Rubens. The museum's collection of works by the great Flemish painter ranks among the world's best both for the number of his own works and their high quality.

The Union of Earth and Water is an allegorical composition. It symbolizes the union of the two elements in the form of two deities: the goddess Cybele and Neptune, the ruler of seas and oceans. The subject of the picture is apparently related to the historical events witnessed by the artist himself. During that period Flanders' outcome to the sea was blocked because of the war, the estuary of the river Scheldt was closed, and this damaged trade and was destructive for the country's economy.

The collection of Dutch painting from the seventeenth and eighteenth centuries is also superb — it includes more than 2,000 paintings and is second only to the Rijksmuseum in Amsterdam as regards the number of artists represented. The gem of the collection are twenty-five masterpieces by Rembrandt. They illustrate different periods of his artistic career.

Danaë is worthy of particular note among works by the mature Rembrandt. The subject of the painting is borrowed from Greek mythology. Acrisius, the king of Argos, having learned from an oracle that he would die from the hand of his grandson, confined his daughter Danaë to an inaccessible tower of brass and guarded her. But Zeus, who fell in love with Danaë, penetrated to the palace in the form of a golden shower. Danaë bore to Zeus a son, Perseus, the future hero, who would kill the Gorgon Medusa.

The masterpiece has a tragic history. In June 1985 a maniac poured sulfuric acid on it. It took twelve years of restorers' careful work to recreate the canvas in all its magnificence again.

This subject was painted by other masters of European painting too, for example by the Flemish artist Jacob Jordaens. The Hermitage owns his *Bean King* or *The King Is Drinking!* depicting a merrymaking company. According to tradition, a large bean was baked in a pie and the one who received it with a piece of pie became the "bean king", that is the sole ruler of the entire company for this party.

The Hermitage has a vast collection of French art which is displayed in more than forty rooms. You can see there many outstanding paintings by French artists, from pieces by unknown fifteenth-century masters to works by contemporary painters. Among master-pieces of seventeenth-century painting are works by the greatest French artist Nicolas Poussin, such as *Tancred and Erminia*, *Descent from the Cross* and *Landscape with Polyphemus*, and by Claude Lorraine, the creator of the "ideal landscape". The brilliant pictures by such outstanding masters as Antoine

Vincent van Gogh. 1853–1890
The Ladies of Arles. **1888**

Henri Matisse. 1869–1954
The Red Room. **1908**

The Twelve-Column Hall in the New Hermitage. 1842–51. Architects Vasily Stasov and Nikolai Yefimov. Designed by Leo von Klenze

The Winter Canal

Watteau, François Boucher, Jean-Baptiste Simeon Chardin, Jean-Baptiste Greuze, Honoré Fragonard and Hubert Robert will introduce you to eighteenth-century French painting. The collection of works from the first half and middle of the nineteenth century is also very rich although not all major artists are equally well represented. The outstanding collection of French painting from the second half of the nineteenth and early twentieth century completes the exhibition. Displayed there are works by Claude Monet, Camille Pissarro, Alfred Sisley, Auguste Renoir, Edgar Degas, Paul Cézanne, Paul Gauguin, Vincent van Gogh, Pierre Bonnard, Albert Marquet, as well as representative collections of paintings by Henri Matisse and Pablo Picasso.

The building of the New Hermitage was designed by Leo von Klenze exclusively for the museum objects. Its first floor was to accommodate an exhibition of painting. The high-vaulted rooms, the so-called Small and Large Skylight Halls, are used to display works by Italian and Spanish artists.

The ground floor houses the collections of classical antique art — white marble sculptures, the collection of black- and red-figure vases, one of the largest in the world, numerous articles of bronze, superb examples of carved gemstones — cameos and intaglios, and terra-cotta statuettes from Tanagra.

One of the rooms, the Twelve-Columned Hall, resembles the interior of a Greek temple. The walls are adorned with painted decorations featuring subjects from classical mythology and reminiscent of paintings on ancient Greek vases, examples of which can be seen in this room.

At the present time the collection of the Hermitage amounts to over two and a half million works of art and artifacts, including 15,000 paintings, over 12,000

Portico of the New Hermitage Atlantes. 1844–49. Sculptor Alexander Terebenev

View of Decembrists' Square from the University Embankment

Monument to Peter the Great (the "Bronze Horseman"). 1774–78. Sculptor Maurice Etienne Falconet

sculptures, more than 600,000 engravings and drawings, over a million of coins and medals. The exhibitions of the museum occupy 350 rooms, their interiors being an appropriate "environment" for masterpieces shown in them.

Senate Square became an important place in St Petersburg already in the 1760s. But its ensemble, like that of Palace Square, took its final shape in the 1840s. Its construction coincided with the facing of the nearby embankment with granite and the building of the wooden St Isaac Bridge that linked the centre of the city with Vasilyevsky Island.

After the Admiralty had been redesigned by Andreyan Zakharov, the necessity to reconstruct the building of

the Senate became evident. The project presented by Carlo Rossi won a competition in which many eminent architects participated. The architect had a difficult task — he had to unite the already existing building of the Admiralty and a monument to Peter the Great. He perfectly solved the task and created a superb architectural work — the two huge buildings of **the Senate and Holy Synod** connected by a beautiful arch.

It is apparent that the focal centre of the square is the monument to Peter the Great, commonly known as the ***Bronze Horseman***. The life-size model of the equestrian statue was produced by the French sculptor Etienne Maurice Falconet. Peter's head was modelled by

Falconet's pupil, Marie Anne Collot. The giant granite boulder (the "Thunder-Stone"), which is carved to imitate a natural rock and serves as a pedestal of the statue, was discovered in 1768 on the shore of the Gulf of Finland, near the village of Lakhta. The delivery of the colossal monolith, weighing 1,600 tons, to the site intended for the monument, was very difficult. The boulder was brought to St Petersburg only in 1770, on a special ship.

Remarkable for its perfect composition and mastery of execution, this monument is justly regarded as one of the utmost accomplishments of monumental sculpture in the eighteenth century. Extremely dynamic in its

way as the spire of the Admiralty and the SS Peter and Paul Cathedral.

Before the 1917 Revolution St Isaac's was the main church of the capital and the principal cathedral of the Empire. It was laid down in honour of Peter the Great and consecrated to his patron saint, St Isaac of Dalmatia, whose feast day (12 June) coincides with the Tsar's birthday. St Isaac's is a great achievement of Russian building techniques — in the process of its construction several very complicated technical and engineering problems were solved. The edifice strikes by its dimensions: its height is 101.5 metres; the dome, 25.8 metres in diameter, is sur-

Outside view of St Isaac's

The Apostle Peter **on the pediment of St Isaac's. 1843–45. Sculptor Ivan Vitali**

silhouette, the *Bronze Horseman* does not repeat ancient or Renaissance models. The figure of Peter the Great is full of grandeur and might; the horse, rearing above the precipice, is very dynamic.

Next to Decembrists' Square, separated from it by Admiralty Prospect, stands **St Isaac's Cathedral**. Its elaborate design and sumptuous and varied decoration contrast with the more clear-cut and austere edifices surrounding the square. St Isaac's, with its overpowering yet somewhat gloomy beauty, is one of the most imposing large-scale structures in St Petersburg. Controversies about this architectural monument have been heard for many decades now. You can doubt its artistic merits, but it is obvious that you cannot imagine the panorama of the Neva banks without its impressive outline. Its powerful dome glistening with gold became a major landmark of the St Petersburg skyline in the same

St Isaac's Cathedral. 1818–58. Architect Auguste de Montferrand

Detail of the iconostasis of St Isaac's

**Detail of the drum and
a pendentive of the main dome of St Isaac's**

rounded by 112 monolithic granite columns, each 17 metres in height and weighing 114 tons, with its walls up to 5 metres thick. The cathedral accommodates up to 12,000 worshippers.

St Isaac's is abundant in sculptural decoration — it is adorned with 350 statues and reliefs by the best Russian sculptors of the middle of the nineteenth century: Ivan Vitaly, Piotr Klodt, Nikolai Pimenov and others.

The interior decor of the cathedral overwhelms visitors by its majesty. The glistening of bronze and gilding and the shimmer of diverse kinds of granite, jasper, porphyry and mosaics merge into a symphony of wealth and luxury. The dozens of mosaics and painted panels, works by the outstanding Russian academy-style painters Karl Briullov, Fiodor Bruni, Piotr Basin and Timofei Neff, are especially impressive.

The building of St Isaac's took more time than the construction of any other cathedral in St Petersburg. Auguste de Montferrand, who devoted a half of his life to the construction of the main cathedral of the Empire, died a month after the ceremony of its inauguration. The architect wanted to be buried in St Isaac's crypt, in keeping with a European age-old custom, but the then reigning Emperor Alexander II did not allow to have the architect buried in the cathedral and his widow carried Montferrand's body to France, his homeland.

St Isaac's became the main formative element for the square which took shape in front of it later and received its name. The Mariinsky Palace was built opposite the cathedral, and at the beginning of

St Isaac Square from the Mariinsky Palace

Monument to Nicholas I on St Isaac Square. 1856–59. Sculptors Piotr Klodt, Nikolai Ramazanov and Robert Zaleman; architect Auguste de Montferrand

the next century the buildings of the Astoria Hotel and the German Embassy completed the ensemble.

The equestrian monument to Nicholas I stands in the centre of the square. Its somewhat excessively detailed decor matches the sumptuous artistic solution of St Isaac's. Thanks to the expressive silhouette of the equestrian statue the monument adds a vivid note to the appearance of the square and perfectly blends with the ensemble.

The Tsar is portrayed in the uniform dress of a colonel of the Mounted Regiment of the Life-Guards (he was its chief), in a helmet with an eagle. The corners of the pedestal are decorated with allegorical female figures, whose faces bear similarity to those of his daughters and consort. The bas-reliefs at the edges of the pedestal illustrate some events from the reign of Nicholas I.

The large equestrian group rests merely on two points of support —

the monument is an example of a rare artistic ingenuity. The horse's croup was filled with a large number of small lead shots and its rear legs were attached to the base of the pedestal by metal rods.

If you walk from the monument to Nicholas I downstream the Moika, you will come to one of the most romantic and majestic sights in St Petersburg on the right bank — the so-called **New Holland Arch**. Concealed in one of the most mysterious parts of the city, it appears suddenly, with its impressive image reflected in the smooth waters of the quiet Moika. The giant arch is flanked by powerful coupled Tuscan columns carrying an entablature, the semicircular vault rests on smaller columns. The structure is made of granite combined with insets of Pudost stone.

It seems paradoxical that this splendid "ruin of past majesty", a beautiful quotation from antiquity, was built as an element of a warehouse building. Along the perimeter of New Holland there are premises for the vertical storage of timber. The arch had a utilitarian purpose — it was designed to lessen the thrust of mast timber on the butt-end walls of the warehouse. This place, which seems to be a preserve now, once was a busy place where ships loaded with timber could be seen passing through the archway into the canal.

Why does this area near the Galley and Admiralty shipyards bear this name? There is a huge number of islands in the delta of the Neva. New Holland occupies two of them. In fact, there is only one island, but in the process of the warehouse construction a reservoir was dug out on it and a canal running to the river divided the island into two parts. The view of slipways, timber warehouses, canals and foreign speech often heard here reminded to Peter the Great his stay in Holland, which was so dear to him, hence the name.

In the early nineteenth century a military prison was built on New Holland and later another building was

The New Holland Arch. 1765–1780s. Architects Savva Chevakinsky and Jean-Baptiste Vallin de la Mothe

The New Holland building at the crossing of the Kriukov and Krustein Canals

The curtain of the Mariinsky Theatre. Designed by Alexander Golovin

Scene from the opera *The Maid of Pskov* by Rimsky-Korsakov staged at the Mariinsky Theatre

The Mariinsky Theatre. 1859–60, architect Albert Cavos; 1883–96, architect Victor Schröter

constructed at the edge of the Kriukov and Krustein Canals.

Not far from New Holland lies Kolomna, a district where poor clerks and craftsmen formerly lived. The territory near it, bordered by the Moika, Kriukov and Griboyedov Canals, is remarkable for another important landmark, Theatre Square. It is divided by Glinka Street, on which two building stand opposite one another — the Conservatoire named after Nikolai Rimsky-Korsakov and **the Mariinsky Theatre** (famous as the Kirov Company in the Soviet period), one of the most famous opera and ballet companies in the world. It played an outstanding role in the development of Russian culture. It was here that many works by the great Russian composers Mikhail Glinka, Modest Mussorgsky and Piotr Tchaikovsky sounded for the first time. Many outstanding people performed on

its stage including the legendary singer Fiodor Chaliapine, brilliant dancers Anna Pavlova, Mikhail Fokine and Vaslav Nijinsky. Galina Ulanova, Rudolf Nureyev and Mikhail Baryshnikov began their creative career in this building. The famous "Kirov Ballet" exerted an undoubted influence on many ballet schools of Europe and America.

The splendid curtain produced according to a design by the outstanding scenographer Alexander Golovin became a symbol of the celebrated company.

Let us return to the central part of the former Admiralty Side. It is from the tower of the Admiralty that the main thoroughfare of St Petersburg, Nevsky Prospect, begins. It ends by the St Alexander Nevsky Lavra crossing the centre of the city.

Nevsky Prospect, however, is not an

arterial road alone — there are lots of monuments around it which are well known to most of Russians.

At the very beginning of Nevsky Prospect, on the left bank of the Moika River, not far from Palace Square, stands the house in which the great Russian poet Alexander Pushkin lived for two years and ended his life. He was brought her mortally wounded at a duel, and people from the entire city came to this house hoping for the best. The poet's heart ceased beating at 2 hours 45 minutes in the afternoon on 29 January 1837. The sad news spread like wildfire all over the capital.

Today, the rooms of **Pushkin's last flat** house a memorial exhibition. The poet's study has been recreated exactly as it was left by the owner. Displayed here are the poet's personal belongings, such as his writing desk, armchair, ink-pot and a stuff with a button from Peter

The Alexander Pushkin Memorial Flat on the Moika

Alexander Pushkin's Study

the Great's camisole set into its handle. There is a great number of books in the study — more than four thousand volumes devoted to various fields of knowledge and in different languages — the poet knew more than ten languages.

At the spot where the Moika crosses Nevsky Prospect there is another notable building, **the Stroganov Palace**. The building owes its name to its former owners, Counts Stroganov, one of the richest and most aristocratic families in Russia. It was built for Count Alexander Stroganov, a highly educated patron of arts, known for his liberal views, a courtier who shone out during the reigns of four emperors — Elizabeth Petrovna, Catherine the Great, Paul I and Alexander I. He became famous in the history of Russian culture as a patron of

The Stroganov Palace. 1752–54. Architect Francesco Bartolomeo Rastrelli

The Kazan Cathedral. 1801–11. Architect Andrei Voronikhin

the former serf, the great architect Andrei Voronikhin, the builder of the Kazan Cathedral, who grew up from his young years in the Stroganov Palace.

The palace was designed by Rastrelli, the famous creator of the Winter Palace. It is a sort of the architect's trial of strength, and a successful one, before the construction of his best work. Although the palace was Stroganov's mansion, it does not conform to the standard estate design — a mansion with wings and a huge court in front of the central building. Its compact arrangement is due to the fact that its main façade overlooks Nevsky Prospect and another one faces the Moika. It has no projecting parts, its space is limited, but the sculptural decoration is lavish and fanciful: the columns are set in

clusters, the pediments are broken and the cornices are adorned with relief decoration. The estate could not be imagined without a courtyard, so an original solution was found — the courtyard was located within the building so that it combined both economical and representative functions serving also as a garden separated from the bustle of nearby street life by a magnificent gate decorated with lion masks.

Not far from the Stroganov Palace is **the Kazan Cathedral**, a building which is a true gem of Nevsky Prospect. It was to the enthusiasm and energy of Count Stroganov that St Petersburg owes the construction of the cathedral, a top achievement of Russian Classicism on a par with the Admiralty built by Zakharov.

The cathedral is a memorial structure. In 1813 Field Marshal Kutuzov, a hero of the 1812 War, was buried here. Housed in the cathedral are also numerous trophies of the war against Napoleon — banners and standards, keys from captured fortresses and towns and Marshal Davout's staff of office. The monuments to Field Marshals Mikhail Kutuzov and Mikhail Barclay de Tolly can be seen on the square in front of the northern façade of the cathedral.

The northern colonnade of the Kazan Cathedral faces Griboyedov Canal which crosses Nevsky Prospect. Not far from the prospect the canal is spanned by **the Bank Bridge** decorated with fanciful sculptures of griffins, mythological winged lions, holding in

The Bank Bridge across the Griboyedov Canal. 1825–26. Engineer Georg Tretter

Griffins on the Bank Bridge. Sculptor Pavel Sokolov

their mouths the chains which support this suspension bridge. The structures of another bridge downstream the Griboyedov Canal, known as **the Lion Bridge**, are also decoratively interpreted. These bridges were put up in 1825–26 and their engineering solutions were the last word in Russian bridge building at that period.

Bridges are an integral part of the architectural look of the "Northern Palmyra", a city of numerous rivers and canals. There are about eight hundred bridges in St Petersburg and its environs. A poetic atmosphere reigns the city during the season of the White Nights in early summer when the Neva bridges are raised to make the passage of ships to the sea possible.

The Lion Bridge across the Griboyedov Canal. 1825–26. Engineers Georg Tretter and Vasily Khristianovich

Lions decorating the Lion Bridge. Sculptor Pavel Sokolov

Let us now return to the place where Nevsky Prospect is crossed by the Griboyedov Canal. At the confluence of the canal with the Moika, there stands, well observed from Nevsky Prospect, **the Cathedral of the Resurrection** which has been recently opened for visitors after many years of restoration. Its commonly used title, **"Our Saviour-on-the-Spilt-Blood"**, commemorates the tragic event of 1 March 1881 when a terrorist threw a bomb and mortally wounded the Tsar, Alexander II. There was literally a "hunt" after the Tsar — six attempts failed before the successful one. The famous Parisian fortune-teller had foretold Alexander II that he would die from the eighth attempt. Since the Tsar was wounded by the second bomb

Detail of the southern façade of the Cathedral of the Resurrection ("Our Saviour-on-the-Spilt-Blood")

The Cathedral of the Resurrection ("Our Saviour-on-the-Spilt-Blood"). 1883–1907. Architects Alfred Parland and Archimandrite Ignaty (Malyshev)

Cupolas of the Cathedral of the Resurrection ("Our Saviour-on-the Spilt-Blood")

thrown at him, it may be considered that the prophecy came true. It must be noted, though, that Alexander II was one of the brightest personalities among the Russian autocrats and perhaps less than anybody deserved such end. He was called the "liberator-Tsar" for his progressive reforms including the liberation of peasants from serfdom they had suffered for many centuries.

A decision was taken to put up a cathedral at the place of assassination. Its interior encompassed that part of the roadway at the edge of the canal which was stained with the Tsar's blood. This accounts for the unusual position of the cathedral. The builders even had to extend the embankment to erect the bell-tower.

The Cathedral of the Resurrection reflects a recourse to national stylistic devices characteristic of Russian architecture in the second half of the nineteenth century. It is apparently largely modelled on the Cathedral of St Basil the Blessed on Red Square in Moscow. The central rectangular volume of the St Petersburg cathedral is typical of Russian churches, with four onion-shaped cupolas around the middle drum completed by a tent-shaped top. The bell-tower is incorporated into the building.

The cathedral is 81 metres high. Its sumptuous decor makes it very attractive. The cupolas are covered with gilded and enamelled

Mosaic: *The Crucifix*. Designed by Alfred Parland

The top of the tent-shaped tower

Mosaic: *The Descent from the Cross*. Artist Vasily Vasnetsov

copper sheets and the roof is decorated with glazed tiles. The exterior is faced with yellow bricks and adorned with coloured tiles placed in recesses; ornamental belts and insets are made of glazed bricks; the walls of the bell-tower bear mosaic representations of provincial coats-of-arms. Set in the niches around the basement are twenty

The southern portal of the Cathedral of the Resurrection ("Our Saviour-on-the-Spilt-Blood")

granite plaques with carved records of outstanding events in the reign of the assassinated Tsar.

The interior of the church adorned with varicoloured Italian marbles and Russian semiprecious stones is even more striking. The canopy, crowned with a rock-crystal cross, is mounted over the place of the tragic death. Its vault is decorated inside with stars made of topazes and other gemstones and rests on four jasper columns. The vaults and walls of the church look like a mosaic carpet.

Mosaics play a major part in the inner and outer decoration of the cathedral. It is a unique accomplishment in the history of world mosaic art remarkable for high artistic merits, virtuoso techniques and vast areas covered with smalt. The overall area of mosaic decoration amounts to 7,500 square metres. The Cathedral of the Resurrection is the only place which can be regarded as a museum of the art of mosaic in Russia.

Next to the cathedral, between the Moika, Griboyedov Canal and Italian Street, stands **the Mikhailovsky Palace** built for Grand Duke Mikhail Pavlovich, brother of Emperor Alexander I.

Carlo Rossi, who supervised the construction of the palace, understood his task much wider. His work on the residence for the grand duke grew into the creation of a whole complex including a magnificent palace, a square with a garden and a system of nearby streets, with numerous dwelling houses. Mikhailovskaya Street, located on the axis of the palace, links the square with Nevsky Prospect. Now it is one of important streets in the city. On its left

The northern portal of the Cathedral of the Resurrection ("Our Saviour-on-the-Spilt-Blood")

Mosaic: *The Pantocrator*. Artist Mikhail Nesterov

Railing of the Mikhailovsky Garden near the Cathedral of the Resurrection ("Our Saviour-on-the-Spilt-Blood")

**The Europe Hotel (1873–75, architect Ludwig Fontana)
at the corner of Nevsky Prospect and Mikhailovskaya Street**

side is the Europe Hotel, the most prestigious hotel in St Petersburg.

The significance of this area is not limited to its wealth of architectural monuments. It is a centre of musical culture and fine arts. Arts Square in front of the palace owes its name to various cultural establishments, such as the Russian Museum, the Philharmonic Society, the Small Opera House and the Theatre of Musical Comedy, located around it. In front of the Mikhailovsky Palace stands a monument to the great poet Alexander Pushkin.

The ensemble of the Mikhailovsky Palace is an outstanding example of Classical architecture. The main façade of the palace behind a huge courtyard with fine railings, the majestic central building next to the austere simplicity of the service block, the grand park façade with an impressive loggia and granite terrace lined with mighty age-old trees, the elegant pavilion by the Moika, the overall extremely interesting layout of the environment of the palace with a perspective view of the square and palace unfolding from Nevsky Prospect — all attracts one's attention and blends together to make up one of the most magnificent sights in the central part of St Petersburg.

The interior decoration of the Mikhailovsky Palace is extremely rich. The grand state staircase of the building occupies its entire central part behind the central portico and equal to it in height. The White Hall is particularly beautiful among the surviving interiors. The windows of this drawing room afford a view of the garden. The hall is divided into three parts by two pairs of columns, between which, along the walls faced with white artificial marble, are placed gilded sofas and armchairs. The interior and the façades were decorated by the eminent Russian sculptors Vasily Demuth-Malinovsky and Stepan Pimenov, both according to designs by Rossi. Carlo Rossi was a universally gifted man — he was responsible not only for the sculptural decor, but also for ornamental painting and even furnishings.

**Arts Square
Monument to Alexander Pushkin. 1957. Sculptor Mikhail Anikushin
The Mikhailovsky Palace (the Russian Museum). 1819–25. Architect Carlo Rossi**

In 1895–98 the Mikhailovsky Palace was redesigned to house the collection of the newly established Russian Museum named after Emperor Alexander III (now the State Russian Museum). The Russian Museum is, along with the Tretyakov Gallery in Moscow, a major collection of Russian art. The museum preserves works of painting, sculpture, graphics and decorative art dating from the eleventh century to the present day. In addition to the Mikhailovsky Palace, the exhibitions of the museum occupy a whole complex of buildings adjoining the palace and several branches scattered in the city.

Icon painting, a traditional form of Russian mediaeval art, is represented in the museum by examples from the twelfth to seventeenth century. The pride of the collection are works by Andrei Rublev and Dionysius, great Early Russian masters of icon painting. They date from the fourteenth and fifteenth centuries, the period marked by the flowering of icon painting. The previous age is represented by some rare examples as during the Tatar-Mongol invasion many art objects were lost. Therefore the twelfth-century icon *The Archangel Gabriel ("Angel with the Golden Hair")*, now in the Russian Museum, deserves a particular attention.

In the eighteenth century Russian culture became more secular and artists began to show more interest in reality and the individual character of man. The portraits by Fiodor Rokotov, Dmitry Levitsky and Vladimir Borovikovsky, which are represented in the Russian Museum as amply as nowhere else, show that eighteenth-century Russian painting could bear a comparison with works by leading contemporary European artists.

Russian academic art is displayed in two interiors, commonly known as "academic" rooms. One of them is also called the "Briullov" Room. Karl Briullov ranks among the most popular

Icon: *Archangel Gabriel ("Angel with the Golden Hair").* **12th century**

Russian artists. An inspired and gifted painter, he maintains a balance between academic convention and realism in his art. Briullov's most famous canvas, *The Last Day of Pompeii*, is devoted to a real historical event — it shows how the ancient town was ruined as a result of an eruption of the volcano Vesuvius in the first century B.C. Portraits form the most valuable part of Briullov's legacy. They feature inhabitants of

luxurious St Petersburg residences, visitors of aristocratic, literary and music salons of St Petersburg portrayed in the glamour of splendid environment, often showing superb psychological characterization.

In the same room you can see the huge canvas *Phryne During the Eleusinian Mystery in Honour of Poseidon* by the later academic painter Henryk Siemiradzki, a Pole by origin.

The White Hall in the Mikhailovsky Palace. Architect Carlo Rossi

Valentin Serov. 1865–1911
Portrait of Countess Olga Orlova, Née Princess Beloselskaya-Belozerskaya. **1911**

Henryk Siemiradzki. 1843–1902 *Phryne During the Eleusinian Mystery in Honour of Poseidon.* 1889

Ilya Repin. 1844–1930 *The Zaporozhye Cossacks Writing a Mocking Letter to the Turkish Sultan.* 1878–91

80

Ivan Aivazovsky. 1817–1900
The Ninth Wave. 1850

Karl Briullov. 1799–1852
The Last Day of Pompeii. 1830–33

Karl Briullov. 1799–1852
Portrait of Princess Elizabeth Saltykova, Née Countess Stroganova. 1841

He treats the ancient subject as a genre scene. The courtesan Phryne, the first beauty of Greece, a model of the sculptor Praxiteles, is shown naked, performing at a feast the role of Aphrodite, who sprung from sea foam. Greeks, in admiration, are greeting her performance. The spectacular scene unfolds against a sumptuous background — a sunlit landscape with sliding shades and a gentle sea.

The large-scale painting *The Ninth Wave*, immediately arresting one's attention, can possibly be considered a favourite picture of the Russian people.

Ivan Aivazovsky, a marine painter who created it, is known all over the world. The artist's favourite subjects are shipwrecks, with people perishing in a struggle against the rioting elements, yet never losing a hope.

Aivazovsky as a Romantic artist took unusual subjects for his paintings, whereas Ilya Repin, an artist of the realist trend, preferred to portray historical events, such as in his painting *The Zaporozhye Cossacks Writing a Mocking Letter to the Turkish Sultan*. This canvas is one of Repin's many works housed in the Russian Museum.

The Zaporozhye Cossacks, Ukrainian brave warriors, write an answer full of spicy jokes to the sultan Mohammed IV who offered them to subjugate to Turkey and join it. A gem of the collection of early-twentieth-century portraiture is the likeness of Countess Olga Orlova by Valentin Serov, the best Russian portrait painter. The portrait seems to be formal and sumptuous at the first glance, but it has subtle grotesque overtones. The beauty of the model and the abundance of accessories enhance the impression of coldness from her haughty glance of a society lioness.

The National Library of Russia. 1828–32. Architect Carlo Rossi

The Zinger Company building (now the House of Books). 1902–04. Architect Pavel Suzor

The Yeliseyev Food Shop. 1901–03. Architect Gavriil Baranovsky

Nevsky Prospect

Another major centre of cultural life in St Petersburg is **the National Library of Russia** on the opposite side of Nevsky Prospect from the Russian Museum. It was also built to the design of Carlo Rossi. Decorative sculpture is again richly used for the decoration of the façade. Between the columns of the loggia Rossi placed the figures of eminent scholars, orators, writers, and philosophers of antiquity: Hippocrates, Demosthenes, Euripides, Homer and others; the attic is surmounted by the figure of Minerva, the goddess of wisdom, the walls are adorned with numerous bas-reliefs.

The National Library of Russia is one of the oldest and richest book repositories of the country. It has an interesting department of early printed books containing very rare examples, a manuscript department where autographs by major Russian writers, musicians and scholars are preserved; valuable ancient Russian and Western European manuscripts are also kept there. Noted Russian scholars and men of literature worked in this library.

The building of the library stands on Ostrovsky Square in the centre of which soars the Alexandrine Theatre, which was erected during the same period. While constructing the theatre, Rossi redesigned the surrounding area. He connected the two newly formed squares, Ostrovsky Square facing Nevsky Prospect and Chernyshev Square overlooking the Fontanka River, by a fine street now bearing his name.

The building of **the Alexandrine Theatre** is one of the most beautiful examples of Russian Classicism. Its majestic loggia and porticoes are vividly accentuated by the long and smooth

The Alexandrine Theatre. 1828–32. Architect Carlo Rossi

Monument to Catherine the Great. 1873. Sculptors Matvei Chizov and Alexander Opekushin

surfaces of the walls enlivened by sculptural and ornamental motifs. The quadriga of Apollo, the patron of the Muses, is set in the middle of the façade, over the attic. The silhouette of this chariot was drawn in detail by Rossi and executed by Stepan Pimenov who worked much for the famous architect.

Rossi Street behind the theatre is a striking achievement of Classicist architecture, attracting and admiring viewers by its harmonious proportions. The Academy of Ballet Art where many dancers were trained is situated on it.

The four corners of **the Anichkov Bridge** spanning the Fontanka at Nevsky Prospect are decorated with famous sculptural groups representing various stages in horse taming. Peter Klodt, their creator, was remarkable among St Petersburg sculptors of the middle of the nineteenth century for his keen sense of unity between sculpture and architecture. The expressive silhouettes of his statuary perfectly harmonize with the bustling motion of Nevsky Prospect and offer a fine view from any point against the impressive background of the river.

Nearby, at the corner of Nevsky Prospect and the embankment, stands **the Beloselsky-Belozersky Palace** representing the second wave of the Baroque in Russia.

Walking along the embankment you will reach **the Summer Gardens** located on the bank of the Neva, on an island formed by the Fontanka, Moika and Swan Canal. The splendid garden is abundant in statues, sculptural groups and busts (mainly produced by Italian sculptors in the late seventeenth and early eighteenth centuries). Now 89 of the original 250 sculptures have survived.

The Beloselsky-Belozersky Palace. 1846. Architect Andrei Stakenschneider

The graceful railing from the Neva side is a fine achievement of the art of landscape gardening. Its unique elegance attracts lovers of beauty from all over the world. On 4 April 1866 an attempt on the life Emperor Alexander II was made nearby.

The Palace of Peter the Great in the corner of the Summer Gardens was not intended for sumptuous receptions or merry parties — designed as a dwelling for the Tsar's family, it does not struck us by its dimensions or wealth of decor.

The Golden Drawing Room in the Beloselsky-Belozersky Palace

Sculptural group on the Anichkov Bridge. 1846–50. Sculptor Piotr Klodt

Allegorical group *Peace and Abundance* in the Summer Gardens. 1722. Sculptor Pietro Baratta

Statue of *Ceres* in the Summer Gardens. Late 17th century. Holland

The main avenue in the Summer Gardens

The Summer Palace of Peter the Great. 1710–12. Architect Domenico Trezzini

Railing of the Summer Gardens. 1770–84. Architect Yury Velten

The Field of Mars

Monument to Alexander Suvorov. 1801. Sculptors Mikhail Kozlovsky and Fiodor Gordeyev (bas-relief); architect Andrei Voronikhin

To the west of the Summer Gardens, separated from it by the Swan Canal, lies **the Field of Mars** which occupies an area of about nine hectares. The area owes its present-day name, received at the turn of the eighteenth and nineteenth centuries, to the famous training and parade grounds near Rome in the Classical times. The use of this name in St Petersburg was due to the erection of the monuments to Alexander Suvorov and Piotr Rumiantsev, great Russian army leaders, in the area (later the monument to Rumiantsev was transferred to Vasilyevsky Island). For two centuries the Field of Mars remained almost a waste land in the centre of the city, dubbed as the "St Petersburg Sahara", because of clouds of dust and sand over it in summer. It was mainly used for military parades, but sometimes it was also a scene of popular merrymaking with roundabouts and theatrical performances. After the monarchy was overthrown, the place was often used for manifestations and meetings. The victims of the February Revolution and the Civil War were buried there. In 1919, a granite tombstone in the form of a square was erected over the common grave, in the centre of which an Eternal Fire, the first in our country, was lit. Today, the Field of Mars is a beautiful blend of the greenery of its parterre garden and the majestic architecture encircling the square. The area is particularly attractive during the White Nights, when numerous jasmines and lilacs are in bloom.

To the south of the Summer Gardens soars **the Mikhailovsky (or Engineers') Castle**. Once the wooden palace of Empress Elizabeth Petrovna stood on this site. Paul I, perhaps the most tragic

The Mikhailovsky (Engineers') Castle. 1797–1800. Architect Vasily Bazhenov and Vincenzo Brenna
Monument to Peter the Great. 1744–46. Sculptor Bartolomeo Carlo Rastrelli

and contradictory figure in Russian history, was born and spend his first years there. After the death of his mother, Catherine the Great, Paul became the Emperor, but he would not like to live in the Winter Palace. He was always gripped by a feeling of danger coming from the secret of his origin. This led to a mistrust and melancholy which dominated the spirits of the "Russian Hamlet", as Paul was often called because of his mother's participation in the murder of his father, Peter III. "I want to die where I was born", Paul declared and a castle safely protected from enemies began to be built by Vincenzo Brenna to designs by Vasily Bazhenov on the site of the former palace. The castle, named in honour of

Detail of the pediment of
the monument to Peter the Great

The Mikhailovsky (Engineers') Castle from the side of the Summer Gardens

the Archangel Michael, had thick walls and was provided with moats and drawbridges. Unlike the austere southern façade, where an equestrian statue of Peter the Great was erected, the northern façade, decorated with statues of *Hercules* and *Flora* and overlooking the Summer Gardens, gave an impression of a vast and rich estate.

Suppressing by its gloomy majesty, the castle, hardly fitting for living, was used by Paul I as his residence only for forty days. During the night of 1 March 1801 he was murdered as a result of a conspiracy.

In 1823 the castle began to house the Main Engineering School which is notable, in particular, for the fact that the writer Dostoyevsky studied there.

The Pestel (St Panteleimon's) Bridge

Ceiling painting *The Triumph of Venus* in the Marble Hall of the Marble Palace. Artist Stefano Torelli

It was in St Petersburg, the administrative centre and the "façade" of the Russian Empire, that splendid Grand Ducal residences, palaces of courtiers and mansions of aristocracy were mainly concentrated.

In the north-western part of the Field of Mars is **the Marble Palace**, one of the best achievements of Early Russian Classicism. It was built for Grigory Orlov, Catherine the Great's favourite and the head of the conspiracy which brought her to the throne. Legend has it that Catherine the Great herself drew a project of the building and showed it to the architect. Anyway, the palace was built in 1768–85 to designs by Antonio Rinaldi. The architect task was to integrate the Marble Palace into the composition of the Palace Embankment and to add finishing touches completing its appearance. The architect perfectly fulfilled the difficult task. The volume of the Marble Palace serves as a balance

The Marble Hall in the Marble Palace. Architect Antonio Rinaldi; sculptors Mikhail Kozlovsky and Fedot Shubin

The Marble Palace. 1768–85. Architect Antonio Rinaldi

**Monument to Alexander III in front of the Marble Palace. 1906–09.
Sculptor Paolo Trubetskoi**

to the mass of the Winter Palace at the other end of the embankment and at the same time blends well with the entire complex of buildings lining the Neva. The palace is one of few buildings in the city which is totally faced with natural stone, granite and marble. The ground floor of the palace is decorated with pinkish-grey granite slabs, while the walls of the first and second floor are faced with pale pink Tyvdia marble.

Only the main staircase and the first tier of the walls of the Marble Hall have retained the original decor.

By the entrance to the palace you can see a monument to Emperor Alexander III by the sculptor Paolo Trubetskoi. It was originally installed on the square in front of the Nikolayevsky (Moscow) Railway Station in 1909. In 1937, however, the monument was dismantled and the equestrian statue was kept in the courtyard of the Russian Museum for a long time.

Not far from the Marble Palace, also on the Palace Embankment, is an

impressive building in the Renaissance style, formerly the Palace of **Grand Duke Vladimir Alexandrovich** and now used as the St Petersburg House of Scientists.

The palace, part of the continuous line of fine buildings on the Palace Embankment, is typical of St Petersburg architecture in the second half of the nineteenth century. The decor of the interior shows a blend of different styles: the Gothic, Renaissance and Neo-Russian elements.

The Palace of Grand Duke Vladimir Alexandrovich (now the House of Scientists). 1867–72. Architect Alexander Rezanov

The State Drawing Room in the House of Scientists

The State Staircase in the House of Scientists

The Yusupov Palace. 1760s, architect Jean-Baptiste Vallin de la Mothe; 1830–38, architect Andrei Mikhailov the Younger

The Yusupov Palace on the Moika is worthy of particular note among the former residences of the Russian aristocracy in St Petersburg. A small stone building, the property of Count Piotr Shuvalov, a prominent political figure in the reign of Elizabeth Petrovna, stood on this site in the eighteenth century. The mansion was then extended and overbuilt by the architect Jean-Baptiste Vallin de la Mothe. In 1830 it was bought by Prince Nikolai Yusupov, one of the richest people of the period. Between 1830 and 1836 the palace was redesigned for him by the architect Andrei Mikhailov the Younger.

In 1858–59 Hyppolito Monighetti completely redesigned several apartments in the palace and created such new interiors as the Turkish Study

and the Moorish Drawing Room. The drawing room was particularly sumptuous. Its walls were covered with white marble inlaid with dark red and blue putty and adorned with gilded panels. The upper parts of the walls were decorated with Arabic calligraphy on a gilded background.

The last owner of the palace was Prince Felix Yusupov. During the night of 17 December 1916 in the basement room of the Yusupov Palace a group of monarchist conspirators murdered the Tsar's notorious favourite Grigory Rasputin.

Several palaces-estates built on the banks of the Fontanka by various architects in the first half of the eighteenth century were similar to the Yusupov Palace in their layout and

general compositional principles. One of them, **the estate of the Counts Sheremetev**, is a unique architectural monument of the eighteenth century, commonly known as the Fontanka House. Fiodor Argunov and Savva Chevakinsky, eminent architects of the period, took part in its creation.

The main façade of the palace still retains some features of the architectural traditions of the Petrine age. They are particularly evident in the flat treatment of the decor.

The interior decoration carried out in the eighteenth century to plans by Fiodor Argunov has not reached us, since the palace was redesigned several times by such well-known architects as Ivan Starov, Giacomo Quarenghi and Andrei Voronikhin. In 1837–40s the entire

The Moorish Drawing Room in the Yusupov Palace. Architect Hyppolito Monighetti and Alexander Stepanov

Reconstruction of the scene of Grigory Rasputin's murder in the basement room of the Yusupov Palace. Wax effigies of Prince Felix Yusupov (Count Sumarokov-Elston) and Grigory Rasputin

interior decor was altered and a fine wrought-iron railing was put up in front of the building. The gates, decorated with the coat-of-arms of the Sheremetev family, were designed by Nicholas Benois in 1867.

The Fontanka House is not only an architectural monument, but is closely associated with the history of Russian culture. Praskovya Zhemchugova-Kovaliova, a celebrated Russian actress, lived there. In 1801 Count Nikolai Sheremetev married her and the former serf became Countess Sheremeteva.

The country estate of Alexander Bezborodko, now within the city, belongs to beautiful examples of Russian architecture from the late eighteenth century. Its layout is also typical of Russian estates of the period, but it is remarkable for its highly unusual appearance.

St Petersburg as a capital of the Orthodox state had a great number

The Bezborodko Dacha. 1773–77. Architect Carlo Rossi

of churches. Unfortunately many of them have not reached us.

The St Alexander Nevsky Monastery of the Holy Trinity was built on the orders of Peter the Great in 1710 to commemorate the victory of the Russian army led by the Novgorodian Prince Alexander over the Swedes on the banks of the Neva in 1240. In 1724 the remains of St Alexander Nevsky were transferred to the monastery. In 1797 the monastery was given the status of the *lavra* or a major Russian Orthodox monastery.

The architect Domenico Trezzini, who created the general layout of **the St Alexander Nevsky Monastery**, also designed the Annunciation Church and the adjacent dwelling premises within it.

In the eighteenth century several noted architects worked in the monastery: Pietro Antonio Trezzini who built the south-eastern wing of the buildings next to the cathedral; Mikhail

Detail of the gate of the Sheremetev Palace with the crest of the Sheremetev family

The Sheremetev Palace. 1750–55. Architect Savva Chevakinsky and Fiodor Argunov

Rastorguyev who designed the Theological College building and the Communion Bread Baking and Metropolitan Blocks, as well as Piotr Yeropkin, Mikhail Zemtsov and, eventually, the outstanding architect Ivan Starov. Starov completed the building of the monastery in 1790 and created the majestic Cathedral of the Holy Trinity, the focal centre of the entire ensemble. A fine example of ecclesiastic architecture of Early Russian Classicism, the cathedral is crowned by a dome resting on a high drum. The overall composition includes two large bell-towers.

The interior of the cathedral is divided into three parts; the wide nave is flanked by Corinthian columns. The vaults and cupola are painted to sketches by Quarenghi and the statues of saints are by the eminent eighteenth-century sculptor Fedot Shubin. The marvellous iconostasis is decorated with pilasters.

Bells of the St Alexander Nevsky Lavra

The Church of the Annunciation in the St Alexander Nevsky Lavra (Monastery). 1717–25. Architect Domenico Trezzini

The semicircular recess with the Holy Gates in the centre is remarkable for the refinement and elegance of its design. The iconostasis is richly adorned with Russian and Italian marbles.

Ivan Starov was also responsible for the design of the formal entrance to the monastery. In the centre of the stone fence is the building of the Gate Church with an arch. Architecturally, it completes the perspective view of Nevsky Prospect integrating the complex of the monastery buildings into the overall scheme of the city.

Immediately behind the arch of the Gate Church, on either side of the passage, are two Necropolises.

The 18th-Century Necropolis is based on the St Lazarus Cemetery intended for the burial of members of the aristocracy and highest officials of the Russian Empire. The first burials were made exclusively on Peter the Great's permission. Here you can

Alexius, the Metropolitan of St Petersburg, Novgorod and Ladoga (now Alexius II, the Patriarch of All Russias)

The Church of St Theodore in the St Alexander Nevsky Lavra. 1740s–1750. Architect Pietro Antonio Trezzini

Inside view of the dome of the Cathedral of the Holy Trinity in the St Alexander Nevsky Lavra

At the turn of the eighteenth and nineteenth centuries, simultaneously with reforms in the Russian army, an attempt was made to refashion the barracks of the troops quartered in St Petersburg. It was then that the barracks of the Izmailovsky Infantry Regiment of the Guards began to be redesigned. Izmailovsky Prospect was built over with single-storey barrack-like buildings. The focal centre of the area was the wooden **Izmailovsky Cathedral of the Holy Trinity**. By 1770 the building became decrepit and the flood of 1824 inflicted such a heavy damage to it that it had to be demolished. The construction of the new Cathedral of the Holy Trinity to the design of

The nave of the Cathedral of the Holy Trinity in the St Alexander Nevsky Lavra

The Cathedral of the Holy Trinity in the St Alexander Nevsky Lavra. 1776–90. Architect Ivan Starov

see the tombs of Peter's sister Natalia Alexeyevna and his associate General Field Marshal Boris Sheremetev. Many prominent figures in Russian science and culture were buried here: the architects Andreyan Zakharov, Andrei Voronikhin, Ivan Starov and Thomas de Thomon, the painters Vladimir Borovikovsky and Sylvester Shchedrin, the world-famous mathematician Leonhard Euler, and the great Russian scientist and poet Mikhail Lomonosov.

The Necropolis of the Masters of Arts was established on the place of the former Tikhvin Cemetery founded in 1823 as the continuation of the Lazarus Cemetery. In the nineteenth century the celebrated figures in Russian culture — the writers Nikolai Karamzin, Vasily Zhukovsky, the composers Mikhail Glinka, Modest Mussorgsky, Alexander Borodin, Alexander Dargomyzhsky and Piotr Tchaikovsky, as well as many well-known masters of fine arts and the theatre — were buried there.

In 1936–39 the cemetery was reconstructed and the remains of many prominent figures in various arts were brought here from other cemeteries.

The (Izmailovsky) Cathedral of the Holy Trinity. 1828–35. Architect Vasily Stasov

The Cathedral of the Resurrection of the Smolny Monastery. 1748–64. Architect Francesco Bartolomeo Rastrelli

Vasily Stasov began in the spring of 1828 and funded personally by Nicholas I, to commemorate him as the commander of the Izmailovsky Regiment.

The might and majestic simplicity of its architectural forms bring to mind associations with the beautiful examples of Novgorod architecture — St Sophia's and the St George Cathedral.

The cathedral is notable for its vast, clear-cut and light interior. The twenty-four slender Corinthian columns easily support the drum of the main cupola which is decorated with caissons bearing moulded rosettes. The small cupolas

View of the complex of buildings of the St Nicholas or Naval Cathedral of the Epiphany.

The St Nicholas or Naval Cathedral of the Epiphany. 1753–62. Architect Savva Chevakinsky

create additional inner space under them. The semicircular iconostasis with six Corinthian columns is rather unusual. The cathedral was consecrated on 25 May 1835. In 1867 the wedding ceremony of Fiodor Dostoyevsky, a great Russian writer, took place in this cathedral.

In 1829 Vasily Starov was made responsible for the completion of **the Smolny Cathedral**, Rastrelli's celebrated creation and one of the most beautiful structures in St Petersburg dating from the age of Elizabeth Petrovna.

His work is an example of the advanced Baroque. The complex solution of the façades, the treatment of

the extending corners by clusters of columns, the richly ornamented window surrounds and the broken semicircular pediments over the entrance are distinctive elements of eighteenth-century Baroque architecture.

Another remarkable monument of Baroque architecture is **the St Nicholas or Naval Cathedral of the Epiphany** designed by Savva Chevakinsky. Elements of ancient Russian church architecture are also used in its composition. The cathedral, consecrated to St Nicholas, a patron saint of sailors, was built on the former parade grounds of the Naval Regiment. The detached four-tiered bell-tower, notable for its

elegance and beauty, is one of the most perfect structures in eighteenth-century architecture.

The appearance of **the St Prince Vladimir Cathedral** suggests a different period in architecture — that of a shift to Classicism. Its construction began in 1766 to plans by Antonio Rinaldi, but in 1772 a fire largely damaged it. The work was resumed in 1783 under the guidance of Ivan Starov.

The use of apparently Baroque architectural forms does not violate the generally austere and restrained façades of the cathedral. It is one of the first examples of five-cupola churches in St Petersburg.

The Chesme Church has a place of its own among ecclesiastical buildings in St Petersburg. Freely interpreting Gothic motifs, its creator, Yury Velten, attained a sense of great harmony and elegance. The church is part of the ensemble of the Chesme Palace. It owes its name to the victory of the Russian Fleet over the Turks at the Chesme Bay in the Aegean Sea in 1770.

In 1910–12 the so-called **Municipal School House** was put up to designs by the architect Alexander Dmitriyev with the participation of the artist Alexander Benois, in the manner of Petrine architecture. Its interiors were also adorned in the same style. Its decor was remarkable for the panels of painted tiles and elaborately shaped fireplaces. Nowadays, the building houses the Nakhimov Naval Cadet School.

In front of the Nakhimov School stands the cruiser *Aurora*, which became famous for its participation in the

The icon of *Our Lady of Kazan* in the St Prince Vladimir Cathedral

The Chesme Church. 1777–80. Architect Yury Velten

The St Prince Vladimir Cathedral. 1783–89. Architect Ivan Starov

The cruiser *Aurora*

Souvenir stalls near the cruiser *Aurora*

Russo-Japanese War of 1905 and especially for its role in the 1917 Revolution.

It is hardly possible to find any other city the environs of which would be so rich in beautiful sights as St Petersburg. And this is especially amazing because all of these suburban residences emerged within a relatively short period of some two centuries. But each of the country residences has a distinct appearance of its own, its well defined individual style.

Building of the Peter the Great Municipal School (now the Nakhimov Naval School). 1910–12. Architects Alexander Dmitriyev and Albert Benois

The Great Palace at Petrodvorets. 1745–55. Architect Francesco Bartolomeo Rastrelli. The Great Cascade

The Throne Room in the Great Palace. 1770s. Architect Yury Velten

Peterhof

The emergence of Peterhof dates from the early eighteenth century, when Peter the Great, along with the construction of the new capital, established a country residence, Peterhof, intended for amusements and modelled on Versailles, the famous residence of the French king Louis XIV. In 1715 the masonry palace was laid down on a hill and the construction of the Monplaisir Palace began. The laying out of the Upper and Lower Parks on the loamy soil prevalent around

The Great Samson (Sea) Canal

Sculptural decoration of the Great Cascade

Fountain: *Samson Tearing Open the Jaws of the Lion*. **1801. Sculptor Mikhail Kozlovsky**

the palace demanded strenuous efforts and large expenses. Fountains, "the soul of gardens", were built in the Lower Park during the laying out of the area. The beauty of the park depends largely on the features of the terrain. The advantageous position of the palace soaring on the natural elevation is emphasized by the two terraces and two large-scale staircases, which are crossed by the Great Cascade with the Sea Canal running to it. The proximity of the sea gives an impression that the fountains were produced by nature itself. The central sculptural group *Samson Tearing Open the Jaws of a Lion* is dedicated to the battle of Poltava, the decisive battle of the Northern War.

The system supplying the Peterhof fountains with water, built in the early eighteenth century, is truly unique. Unlike Western European parks where water is supplied with the help of machines, engineers have employed at Pavlovsk the natural downward slope of the terrain towards the sea. The thrust

The Monplaisir Palace in the Lower Palace at Petrodvorets. 1714–23. Architects Johann Friedrich Braunstein, Jean-Baptiste Le Blond and Niccolo Michetti

of water is so powerful that the jet of the central fountain spurts out for 22 metres.

The earliest structure in the Lower Park is the Palace of Monplaisir built for Peter the Great. The brick single-storeyed building, with its wide tent-shaped roof and windows of small panes provided with shutters and transoms, looks like houses from paintings by old Dutch masters.

It was not by chance that Peter the Great chose this site for his residence — it recalled Holland to him. The cosy palace afforded fine views of the subdued sea — the Tsar could watch war and trade ships passing by to St Petersburg or the sights of the newly built fort of Kronstadt.

The Hall in the Palace of Monplaisir

The Cathedral of the SS Apostles Peter and Paul. 1895–1905. Architect Nikolai Sultanov

Tsarskoye Selo

This royal residence is located on the high hill dominating the surroundings. Earlier a small farmstead known as the *Saari-mojs* ("high place"), was on this site. In 1711, it was presented to Catherine together with five other former Swedish estates. Thus the foundation was laid for the magnificent country estate which would be the main residence of the Imperial court for a long time.

The compositional centre of the palace and park complex of Tsarskoye Selo is the Great Catherine Palace. Many well-known architects took part in its creation completed by the celebrated

**Cupolas of the Church of
the Great Catherine Palace**

The Great Catherine Palace at Tsarskoye Selo. 1751–56. Architect Francesco Bartolomeo Rastrelli

Rastrelli. The façade of the palace stretching for 300 metres produced a striking impression by its unusually sumptuous shapes, a play of light and shade on its numerous columns and semi-columns, projections, atlantes and caryatids, its abundant carved decoration and the light of its huge windows. The palace is a brilliant achievement of the Elizabethan Baroque.

The interior of the Great Palace is no less magnificent. By piercing the walls with windows along their entire length and by covering the intervals with mirrors in gilded frames, the architect achieved a striking effect

**The Egyptian Gate. 1827–30.
Architect Adam Menelaws**

**The Bedroom in the Great Catherine Palace. 1781–82, architect Charles Cameron;
1820s, architect Vasily Stasov**

of immateriality. The apartments adjacent to the central hall are also lavishly decorated.

The terrace resting on vaults connects the palace with a group of structures executed in the Classical style which are known by the name of their designer — the Quarenghi Terms.

The earliest part of the Catherine Park is the Old Garden laid out in the regular manner in the early eighteenth century. Its concept belonged to Jan Roosen, the designer of the Summer Gardens. In the 1770s the garden was substantially altered. The trees were no longer cropped since that period and towards the end of the century the formal and landscape parts of the Catherine Park merged together.

The Cameron Gallery. 1783–86. Architect Charles Cameron

The Great Hall in the Agate Pavilion. 1780s. Charles Cameron

View of the Great Lake. The Chesme (Rostral) Column. 1771–76. Architect Antonio Rinaldi

The Palladian (Marble) Bridge in the Catherine Park. 1772–74. Architect Vasily Neyelov

**The Great Palace at Pavlovsk. 1782–86, architect Charles Cameron;
1796–99, architect Vincenzo Brenna**

Pavlovsk

In 1777 Catherine the Great presented a plot of land to her son Paul and his wife Maria Fiodorovna, to commemorate the birth of their son (the future Emperor Alexander II). It was situated not far from Tsarskoye Selo, on the banks of the Slavianka River. In 1781, Charles Cameron, who was invited to build the Great Palace in 1781, completed it in 1786.

The main block of the palace, a three-storeyed building with a dome resting on 64 small columns, is remarkable for the clarity and simplicity of its architectural layout. The staircase leads from the entrance hall to state rooms, among which the Grecian Hall modelled on ancient multi-columned courtyards is worthy of particular note. The rectangular hall is embellished with wooden columns faced with artificial marble. The columns have a purely decorative function — they are not only devoid of any load but

The Bedroom belonging to Maria Fiodorovna's apartments in the Great Palace. 1796–99, architect Charles Cameron

The Lantern Study in the Great Palace. 1807.
Architect Andrei Voronikhin

The Boudoir in the Great Palace. 1792.
Architect Vincenzo Brenna

View of the western façade of the Great Palace and the Centaur Bridge

The Grecian Hall in the Great Palace. 1803. Architect Andrei Voronikhin

are even "suspended" from the ceiling. Hanging on long chains are white marble lamps made in imitation of Pompeian models.

One of the most magnificent rooms of the palace is the State Bedroom belonging to the apartments of Maria Fiodorovna. Its decor and furnishings were largely inspired by the impressions the princely couple had during their travel to Europe, in particular morning receptions in the bedroom of the French king Louis XVI in the Versailles Palace.

One of the most graceful rooms in the palace is the so-called Lantern Study. The interior owes its name to the semicircular glazed projection separated from the room by an arch which rests on caryatids produced by the sculptor Vasily Demuth-Malinovsky. The furniture was designed by Andrei Voronikhin. The abundance of flowers and a beautiful sight of Her Majesty's Own Garden unfolding from the Lantern Study lend a special charm to this interior.

It took about a half of a century, approximately from 1780 to 1828, for the creation of the Pavlovsk Park. All changes in landscape gardening traditions from the late eighteenth to the early twentieth centuries can be traced in it. The Pavlovsk Park is one of the world's best examples of the English style of landscape gardening, but at the same time the peculiarities of the Russian scenery have been taken into account.

The Apollo Colonnade, the Temple of Friendship and other characteristic structures of the Pavlovsk Park were designed by Charles Cameron. The Temple of Friendship, reminiscent of ancient Greek monuments, was built as an expression of gratitude to Catherine the Great for the presentation of Pavlovsk. The choice of a site for this extremely harmonious and exquisite structure has been very successful — it perfectly blends with clusters of trees, fields and splendid vistas of the Slavianka banks.

126

The Apollo Colonnade. 1782. Architect Charles Cameron

The Temple of Friendship. 1780. Architect Charles Cameron

Санкт-Петербург

Альбом (на английском языке)

Издательство «Альфа-Колор»
Санкт-Петербург. 1998
ЛР № 063313, 28 февраля 1994

Цветоделение AMOS St. Petersburg

PRINTED AND BOUND IN FINLAND